THE LITTLE GUIDE TO
BIRDS

THE LITTLE GUIDE TO
BIRDS

Illustrations
by Tom Frost

Words by
Alison Davies

Hardie Grant

QUADRILLE

Introduction

The world of birds contains an abundance of colour and magic, an enchanting realm where even the smallest species has something special to offer, from the ornately crafted shape of their tail feathers to a fiery crown and beyond. Whether dull or bright, each bird has a gift to share, and it's all here in this book.

Should you need further convincing, look to the images carefully laid out on each page, the way the prints resonate, taking the essence of each creature and capturing it in one perfect moment. You'd be forgiven for thinking they might come to life in a flurry of gossamer wings, taking flight from paper to air in a heartbeat. Combine this with the scientific information and description and you'll be able to build a picture of each bird's environment, how they live and the skills and talents that make them unique.

The element of folklore adds another dimension to this avian kingdom; ancient whispers and threads of stories from around the world help you see why we've been fascinated with birds for centuries. We've given them names and attributes, linked them to the gods, and even considered them supernatural in status and power. Winged messengers, they traverse the skies, and even those that prefer the safety of dry land intrigue us.

There's also an informative spotter's guide at the back so that you can see and experience them for yourself. Let the pictures and words take you on a journey, and prepare to be amazed as you explore this feathery domain.

I want to sing like the birds sing, not worrying about who hears or what they think.

RUMI

Sparrowhawk

Accipiter nisus

WINGSPAN 59–80cm (24–31in) / 28–38cm (11–15in)
NUMBER OF EGGS 3–6 each clutch
HABITAT Woods with dense cover next to hunting grounds
(mixed woodland, fields, gardens and parks)
DISTRIBUTION All of Europe, except Iceland
FOOD Mostly small birds (up to the size of a wood pigeon), sometimes bats
MALES AND FEMALES Females are larger than the males, with grey-brown
backs rather than grey-blue and more obvious, darker barring on their chests

Capable of flying up to 50kph (30mph), Sparrowhawks often ambush flocks of small birds like tits and sparrows, flying fast and low to take them by surprise. The females will also determinedly hunt down larger birds such as wood pigeons. Hawks have long been associated with the gods. In Greek mythology, they were linked to Jupiter, the king of the gods. In ancient Egypt, Horus the Egyptian Sky God, was represented by a hieroglyph in the shape of this striking bird. Interestingly, folklore around the world often attributes the cry or appearance of a hawk as an omen of death.

Mandarin

Aix galericulata

WINGSPAN 65–75cm (26–30in) / 45cm (18in)
NUMBER OF EGGS 9–12 each clutch
HABITAT Wetlands and park lakes
DISTRIBUTION East Asia, Eastern Russia, UK, Ireland,
parts of Europe; there's also a small population in the US
FOOD Aquatic plants, seeds, acorns, grains and insects
MALES AND FEMALES Males are much more colourful,
with more elaborate plumage than the females

Native to parts of Asia, this striking duck spread to other parts of the
world by escaping from captivity (or being released). Unmistakable
because of its colourful feathers and beautiful orange cheek plumes,
you may be lucky enough to see this shy bird on rivers and lakes. In
Japanese and Chinese folklore, Mandarin ducks are often potrayed
as human lovers who have been cruelly separated. In reality, these
gorgeous creatures mate for life, and perform intricate synchronised
swimming routines to illustrate that they are totally
in tune with each other.

Common Kingfisher

Alcedo atthis

WINGSPAN 24–26cm (10in) / 16–17cm (7in)
NUMBER OF EGGS 2–3 clutches of 2–10 eggs
HABITAT Lakes, streams, canals, ponds and rivers
DISTRIBUTION Throughout Europe, North Africa, Asia
FOOD Fish, aquatic invertebrates, amphibians
MALES AND FEMALES Similar but male's bill is all black and female's is black with a reddish orange lower beak

Unmistakable with its electric-blue and orange plumage, you might spot a kingfisher as it whizzes along the waterside from perch to perch, watching for fish below. With more than 87 different species of kingfisher worldwide, it's no wonder this glorious bird features in numerous myths and legends. According to the ancient Greeks, kingfishers built their nests on a raft of fish-bones and floated them on the sea. The gods made sure that the seas and winds were calm during this period, which occurred just after winter solstice. This is where the term 'halcyon days' originates from, as the Greek name for kingfisher is *halcyon*.

Honduran Emerald Hummingbird

Amazilia luciae

WINGSPAN 9.5cm (4in)
NUMBER OF EGGS Unknown, although research suggests 1–2 each clutch
HABITAT Dry thorn forest and scrub
DISTRIBUTION Only found in parts of Honduras
FOOD Small insects and nectar
MALES AND FEMALES The female is much duller in colour than the male

Extremely rare, the endangered Honduran emerald hummingbird zips through the air at top speed. Gone in the blink of an eye, this glistening jewel is like an acrobat, catching insects in mid-air and sipping nectar from up to 2000 flowers per day. These tiny birds can take up to 500 breaths per minute and have the highest oxygen intake of any vertebrate. Loss of habitat is the main threat to its survival. In folklore, it is generally considered a good omen and a symbol of joy.

Emperor Penguin

Aptenodytes forsteri

WINGSPAN 76–89cm (30–35in) / 115cm (45in)
NUMBER OF EGGS 1 each year
HABITAT Compact ice on the Antarctic continent and the ocean
DISTRIBUTION Antarctica
FOOD Fish, krill, squid
MALES AND FEMALES Identical

The tallest of all types of penguin, the emperor is aptly named. A gifted swimmer, it travels at high speeds and, like dolphins, has the ability to leap out of the water while on the move. The only animals to breed in the Antarctic winter, penguins have evolved special physical adaptations (four layers of tightly compacted feathers and considerable fat) to cope with the harsh conditions. Emperors have also developed special behaviours, such as huddling together to keep warm; it is the only species of penguin that isn't territorial. A convivial companion with a highly sociable nature, once it finds its perfect partner, the emperor will mate for life.

Kiwi

Apteryx australis

WINGSPAN c.40cm (16in)
NUMBER OF EGGS 1–2 each clutch
HABITAT Forest and dense woodland, mountain slopes
DISTRIBUTION New Zealand
FOOD Worms, spiders, insects, seeds and berries
MALES AND FEMALES Females are larger than males

The Latin word *apteryx* means 'without wings' and these little birds are considered honorary mammals in their native New Zealand. With feathers like hair and nostrils at the end of their beaks, the nocturnal kiwi belongs to an ancient group of birds known as the ratites. Curiously wonderful, their evolutionary design cannot be matched. They have evolved to survive in a habitat normally occupied by mammals, which makes them feisty and strong. With a formidable charge, these bird ninjas use their severely sharp claws to defend their territory from attack, and can run as fast as a human.

Grey Heron

Ardea cinerea

WINGSPAN 155–175cm (61–69in) / 90–98cm (36–39in)
NUMBER OF EGGS 4–5 each clutch
HABITAT Grassland, forests, woods, parks, near lakes, rivers and by the coast
DISTRIBUTION Throughout Eurasia and Africa
FOOD Fish, amphibians, small mammals, sometimes small birds and insects
MALES AND FEMALES Identical

These willowy birds often look like feathered statues as they stand motionless in the middle of fields (in areas known as 'standing grounds') and they will often stand stock still for long periods by water watching out for prey. Grey herons aren't fussy about where they find their food and will take fish from garden ponds given the chance. Being long and lithe and with a loud, ghostly call, they attracted superstition in the past. Anglers once believed that their feet gave off a scent which would entice fish near, and it was common to carry a heron's foot for good luck on fishing expeditions.

Shoebill

Balaeniceps rex

WINGSPAN 230–260cm (90–102in) / 115cm (45in)
NUMBER OF EGGS 1–3 each year
HABITAT Fresh water swamps and marshes
DISTRIBUTION Eastern tropical Africa
FOOD Amphibians, carrion, reptiles (including young crocodiles), molluscs and fish (especially lungfish)
MALES AND FEMALES Males and females are similar

The shoe-shaped bill of this aptly-named strange-looking bird is put to good use – plunged deep in the water, it can keep a firm grip on slippery prey and can even decapitate crocodiles. Shoebills rarely make a sound, although they do practise loud 'bill clattering' as a form of communication and greeting. The young birds also make a hiccupping sound when begging for food. Almost prehistoric in appearance, the shoebill was well-known to the ancient Egyptians. Its image is often found adorning tomb walls and on scavenged relics.

Grey Crowned Crane

Balearica regulorum

WINGSPAN 180–200cm (71–79in) / 104cm (41in)
NUMBER OF EGGS 2–3 each clutch
HABITAT Wetlands and grasslands, plains, marshes, rivers and savannah
DISTRIBUTION Eastern and southern Africa
FOOD Insects, lizards, amphibians, fish, grass, nuts and seeds
MALES AND FEMALES Male's are slightly larger, but otherwise identical

The national bird of Uganda, the grey crowned crane is
named for the sharp golden feathers which adorn its head.
This eye-catching headdress makes it stand out from the
crowd, and unlike other cranes, it also prefers to roost in trees.
Slender but statuesque, with a loud honking call, these birds
are the most primitive of their family group, dating back to
the Eocene period. According to research, 11 different types of
crowned crane once existed in Europe and North America, but
these died out as the Earth cooled. Only the warm climate of
Africa provides the perfect environment for this majestic crane.

Bohemian Waxwing

Bombycilla garrulus

WINGSPAN Up to 33cm (13in) / 18cm (7in)
NUMBER OF EGGS 5–6 each clutch
HABITAT Coniferous and mixed forests, gardens, parklands and cities
DISTRIBUTION North America, Northern Europe and parts of Asia
FOOD Berries and insects
MALES AND FEMALES Males and females are similar but males
have longer crests and a more defined throat patch

The gypsy of the bird world, Bohemian waxwings were named because of their nomadic lifestyle, often flying long distances in search of food in winter. The name 'waxwing' comes from the red tips to their wing feathers, which look like drops of sealing wax. Highly sociable, they feed in large groups and take turns to feast on berries. Male and female waxwings often pass a berry back and forth during courtship. Because they're so often on the move, they have no need to defend a territory and have no true song instead they noisily buzz and trill.

Eagle Owl

Bubo bubo

WINGSPAN 131–200 cm (52–79in) / 60–75cm (24–30in)
NUMBER OF EGGS 2–4 each year
HABITAT Forests, deserts and rocky landscapes
DISTRIBUTION North Africa, Europe, Asia, Middle East
FOOD Mainly mammals (rats, mice, foxes, rabbits), other birds (crows, ducks, seabirds, and other birds of prey) and also snakes, lizards, frogs, fish and crabs
MALES AND FEMALES Females are heavier than males and have a higher-pitched call

With its magnificent appearance and haunting call, the eagle owl is often called king among birds. This large owl needs a territory of about 10km (6 miles) to hunt for prey and its hoots can be heard up to distances of 5km (3 miles). In France, they were held in such high esteem they were called *hibou grand-duc*, suggesting they were on a par with dukes, who were the only nobles allowed to wear plumes of their feathers during the Middle Ages. Other cultures revered owls for their wisdom while some, like the ancient Romans, believed that the arrival of the owls inside the city walls was a ominous sign.

Wilson's Bird of Paradise

Cicinnurus respublica

WINGSPAN c.16cm (6in)
NUMBER OF EGGS Clutch size uncertain
HABITAT Hill forests, montane forests and lowland rainforests
DISTRIBUTION Restricted to West Papuan islands
of Waigeo and Batanta in Indonesia
FOOD Small insects and fruit
MALES AND FEMALES The female is less ornate and brownish,
and lacks the bright colours and spiral tail feathers of the male

The male of this species prepares a special arena in which to display his glorious plumage by clearing away any leaves or debris. Before taking centre stage, he ensures maximum sunlight so that he can show off his beautiful colours, including his large emerald breast shield and blue bald head, to the best effect. The female perches above looking down onto the male's vivid and complex display. Bird of paradise plumage was prized for local headdresses, but these days headdresses are passed down through generations and birds are no longer targeted for their feathers.

Common Cuckoo

Cuculus canorus

WINGSPAN 58cm (23in) / 32–34cm (12–14in)

NUMBER OF EGGS Up to 25 each season in different nests

HABITAT Forests and woodlands, forest edges and clearings, meadows, marshes and reedbeds, cultivated areas with trees and bushes

DISTRIBUTION Europe, Asia to Nepal southwards China and Japan. It winters in Africa, crossing the Sahara to reach the equatorial regions, and South Africa

FOOD Insects (especially hairy caterpillars), sometimes the eggs and nestlings of songbirds

MALES AND FEMALES Males and females are similar, but only the male calls 'cuckoo'

Cuckoos are most well-known for laying their eggs in other birds' nests. A female will wait until the coast is clear in the nests of birds like reed warblers, fly in, tip out an egg and replace it with one of her own, leaving the hapless parents to raise her chick. Associated with the Greek goddess Hera, the cuckoo is also known for its sorrowful voice, which in many countries symbolises lost love. According to legend, the god Zeus transformed into the form of a lifeless cuckoo. The goddess Hera took pity on the poor bird, pulling it close to her chest, at which point Zeus returned to his usual shape and seduced her.

Mute Swan

Cygnus olor

WINGSPAN 200–240 (79–95in) / 145–160cm (57–63in)
NUMBER OF EGGS 4–10 each year
HABITAT Along the banks of rivers, lakes, marshes, swamps and parks
DISTRIBUTION Europe, Russia to Arctic, North America, China
FOOD Insects, water plants, seeds, grains and snails
MALES AND FEMALES Males tend to be heavier than the females and have larger black basal knob above bill

These graceful white beauties are the ballerinas of the bird world. Serene upon the surface, they glide with ease and bring love, loyalty and magic to any lakeside scene. Males (known as cobs) and females (known as pens) mate for life and have become a symbol of fidelity. They were also sacred to the Greek goddess Aphrodite. The British Crown Estate has rights over swans in England and Wales and the annual tradition of swan-upping continues to this day, where all the swans are counted and marked.

Great Spotted Woodpecker

Dendrocopos major

WINGSPAN 34–39cm (14–19in) / 22–23cm (9in)
NUMBER OF EGGS 4–7 each clutch
HABITAT Woodlands, parks and gardens
DISTRIBUTION Throughout Europe, North Africa, parts of Asia to Japan
FOOD Insects, larvae, nuts and berries, sometimes eggs and nestlings
MALES AND FEMALES Male has a red patch on his nape, otherwise similar

The well-named woodpecker drums on bark in spring to establish a territory and attract a mate; they also hammer into wood to reach food within. You might think all this head-banging would cause serious damage but they have amazing shock-absorbers in their skulls to protect their brains from injury. The woodpecker was seen as a creature of fortitude and a sign of opportunity: in Greek and Roman mythology, the first king of Latium, Picus, was transformed into a woodpecker by the vengeful witch Circe because he scorned her amorous advances. This striking bird also has associations with Mars the god of war, which only serves to aid its tenacious reputation in folklore.

Robin

Erithacus rubecula

WINGSPAN 20–22 cm (8–9in) / 14cm (5in)
NUMBER OF EGGS 2–3 clutches of 4–6 eggs
HABITAT Woodlands, hedgerows, parks and gardens
DISTRIBUTION Across Europe, east to western Siberia and south to North Africa
FOOD Insects, worms, spiders, small berries and seeds
MALES AND FEMALES Almost identical (NB young birds lack the orange breast)

With its orange-red chest puffed to perfection, the robin is a characterful bird and a symbol of charity. It's one of the few birds that sings all year round (apart from when it moults in late summer) because it is highly territorial. An emblem of Christmas, according to Christian folklore it gained its colourful plumage trying to help Christ on the cross. While attempting to prize a nail loose a few drops of blood stained its breast, changing its appearance for eternity. Despite this act of kindness, the robin was seen as an omen of doom if it entered a home.

Atlantic Puffin

Fratercula arctica

WINGSPAN 47–63cm (19–25in) / 26–29cm (10–11in)
NUMBER OF EGGS 1 each year
HABITAT Rocky coasts and open ocean
DISTRIBUTION Found in eastern North America, Arctic fringes and northwest Europe
FOOD Small fish (sand eels, herring), crustaceans, molluscs
MALES AND FEMALES Males and females are very similar in appearance

Sometimes called 'sea parrots' or 'clowns of the sea' because of the vivid hues of their beak, Atlantic puffins spend about half of the year out at sea where their beaks lose their bright colours. They only come to land to breed in spring, when their plumage and beaks are at their most smart and colourful and this is when you're more likely to see them. Swift fliers, they can reach up to speeds of 88kph (55mph) in the air. They are also expert divers and swimmers, diving up to 60m (200ft) to fish. Males and females play an equal part in incubating their single egg, nesting in burrows or crevices on clifftops.

Jay

Garrulus glandarius

WINGSPAN c.55cm (22in) / 35cm (14in)
NUMBER OF EGGS 5–7 per clutch
HABITAT Mixed woodlands, parks and gardens
DISTRIBUTION Europe and Asia
FOOD Nuts (especially acorns), seeds, berries,
occasionally small mammals, birds and eggs
MALES AND FEMALES Very similar in appearance

It's no surprise that the Gaelic name for this stunning bird is *schreachag choille*, which means 'screamer of the woods' and the Latin name means 'noisy/chattering' and 'of acorns'. It buries a huge stash of acorns in autumn to retrieve later in winter. A jay's shrill screech can be heard reverberating through the treetops, but this is one of many alarm calls that this species has perfected over time. A skilled mimic, it can copy other birds and has been known to mimic mechanical sounds too. This member of the crow family is clever and inquisitive, and a symbol of creative intelligence throughout the world.

Bald Eagle

Haliaeetus leucocephalus

WINGSPAN 183–228cm (72–90in) / 76–94cm (30–37in)
NUMBER OF EGGS 1–3 each year
HABITAT Coastal or forested areas, by rivers, lakes, marshes
DISTRIBUTION Canada, Alaska, United States and northern Mexico
FOOD Fish (especially salmon), birds, reptiles, amphibians,
invertebrates and mammals
MALES AND FEMALES Almost identical but males are smaller

Majestic and powerful, as the bald eagle soars its white head feathers catch the light of the sun, giving it its name. While there's no doubt that its looks are impressive, this eagle is also a clever character and will often harass other birds for their catch rather than hunting itself. The national emblem of the United States since 1782, it's no surprise this enormous bird inspired so much folklore. Native Americans consider it a sacred creature with powerful medicine. Some tribes believe it is the king of the birds, while others see it as a spirit messenger, passing between worlds and communicating with humans and the Creator.

Swallow

Hirundo rustica

WINGSPAN 30–35cm (12–14in) / 17–19cm (7in)
NUMBER OF EGGS 4–8 each clutch
HABITAT Fields, meadows, shorelines, marshes
DISTRIBUTION Around the world, except Antarctica
FOOD Insects, particularly large flies
MALES AND FEMALES Male and females are very similar
in appearance but males have longer tail streamers

With glossy metallic-blue upper-parts and distinctive forked tail streamers, the graceful swallow is easy to spot. Supremely agile, it manoeuvres at speed and feeds on the wing. According to folklore, the sight of a swallow in flight means summer is on the way, but if it is flying low, then it brings rain. If it enters the home, it brings a wealth of good fortune. Better still, if it builds a nest in the roof, this protects the dwelling and all those in it from fire, storms and general bad luck. Up until the 19th century, it was thought that swallows hibernated in the mud at the bottom of ponds, but we now know it migrates thousands of miles to warmer climes.

Himalayan Black-lored Tit

Machlolophus xanthogenys

WINGSPAN c.14cm (5in)

NUMBER OF EGGS 3–5 each clutch

HABITAT Forested areas and edges, plantations, gardens

DISTRIBUTION Areas around the Himalayas

FOOD Insects, spiders and sometimes fruit

MALES AND FEMALES Females have a greyish-olive crest
and mantle and are duller than the males, who have brown
backs and more obvious, darker barring on their chests

With a broad black line down its yellow front, the
black-lored tit is easy to identify. A stunning bird,
with a large and somewhat punky style of crest, it has
a distinctive cry which sounds like 'chi-chi-chi'. It will
nest in woodpecker or barbet holes, or commandeer
manmade shelters, or sometimes makes its own.

Budgerigar

Melopsittacus undulatus

WINGSPAN 25–35cm (10–14in) / 18cm (7in)
NUMBER OF EGGS 4–6 each clutch
HABITAT Open woodland, scrubland and grassland near water
DISTRIBUTION Australia
FOOD Seeds, insects and berries
MALES AND FEMALES Males and females almost identical

One of the smallest parrot species in the world, this diminutive but perfectly formed bird, with its array of colours, is highly prized as a pet. Extremely vocal, its pretty song and ability to mimic are also attractive traits. In the wild, budgies are highly nomadic, robust characters gathering into flocks to roam in search of food. They do not build nests, but prefer to lay their eggs in holes that they find in trees. Cheeky and characterful, the budgerigar is seen by Aboriginals as a symbol of fun and freedom; its common name derives from the Aboriginal name *betcherrygah*.

Bee-eater

Merops apiaster

WINGSPAN 36–40cm (14–16in) / 25–27cm (10in)
NUMBER OF EGGS 6–7 each clutch
HABITAT Open landscapes, forest, scrubland, savannah and marshy terrain
DISTRIBUTION Throughout southern Europe, Africa and Asia
FOOD Bees, wasps, dragonflies and other flying insects
MALES AND FEMALES Males have longer tail spikes
and females have slightly duller plumage

With its rich chestnut crown, and striking blue-green plumage with golden amber hues, the bee-eater commands attention. This gloriously coloured bird feeds on bees and wasps, and while most might avoid a creature that stings, the bee-eater despatches it swiftly. Returning to its perch, it strikes the bee on the head, then wipes the sting free from its abdomen (although it sometimes eats the sting, too). When nesting in holes in sandy banks, the birds have a 'helper' system, whereby more than two adult birds are on hand to feed the chicks. These helpers are male and usually related to the breeding pair.

House Sparrow

Passer domesticus

WINGSPAN 21–25cm (8–10in) / 15cm (6in)
NUMBER OF EGGS 3–5 each clutch
HABITAT Rural areas, allotments, gardens, farmland
DISTRIBUTION Europe, Africa, Asia, North America and Australia
FOOD Mostly seeds and scraps, sometimes nuts, berries, buds and insects
MALES AND FEMALES Males have a grey cap and black bib;
females have a pale stripe above their eyes and are drabber

It's no surprise these bold and boisterous, little birds thrive in occupied areas. Resourceful to the tips of their feathers, they make the most of any scraps they can find and live off the kindness, and sometimes wastefulness, of humans. Despite their friendly nature, European folklore depicted them as omens of doom; if one flew into the home, impending death was certain. The Greeks, on the other hand, associated this charming bird with the goddess Aphrodite, which linked it to spiritual love. Today the sparrow is a welcome visitor to most gardens and sure to raise a smile with its joyful chirruping.

Peacock

Pavo cristatus

WINGSPAN 140–160cm (55–63in) / up to 230cm (90in), including the train

NUMBER OF EGGS Usually 4–6 each clutch, although they can lay up to 12

HABITAT Open forest habitats, grasslands; often kept in gardens and zoos

DISTRIBUTION Native to South Asia but introduced to other parts of the world, including Britain and North America

FOOD Amphibians, reptiles, insects, worms, leaves, roots, seeds, flowers and grains.

MALES AND FEMALES Males are larger and more brightly coloured, with long trains

Flamboyant and ornamental, long train feathers, which they fan when displaying to females, ensure that male peacocks stand out from the crowd. In Europe, they are seen as an ill omen, their luminous feather 'eyespots' likened to the evil eye, a sinister and ominous symbol. In China, the reverse is true: the peacock is treasured as a creature of great dignity. Hindu mythology considers it to be a magical and highly sacred bird and it's generally thought that when the peacock dances, rain will fall.

Grey Partridge

Perdix perdix

WINGSPAN 48cm (19in) / 29–31cm (11–12in)
NUMBER OF EGGS 10–20 each clutch
HABITAT Farmland, wasteland, hedgerows, woodland verges, moors and heaths
DISTRIBUTION Native to Northern Europe and Britain
FOOD Plants, grasses, grain and weed seeds and some insects
MALES AND FEMALES Females are slightly smaller and duller than
the males and the horseshoe shape on the breast is less distinct

A sociable bird, often seen in large groups (known as coveys),
the grey partridge's reputation is far from dull. According to the
Ancients, a partridge on the doorstep meant a sudden death within
the family. If one was seen flying over the house, it would soon
burn. Preparing the bird for cooking was also fraught with danger.
The partridge should be plucked while warm and hung up by its left
leg, otherwise it would bring bad luck. Its population has declined
so much in recent years that it is now on the IUCN's (International
Union for Conservation of Nature) Red List of threatened species.

Greater Flamingo

Phoenicopterus roseus

WINGSPAN 140–170cm (55–67in) / 125–145cm (49–57in)
NUMBER OF EGGS 1 each year
HABITAT Coastal lagoons, saline lakes, estuaries and muddy beaches
DISTRIBUTION Southern Europe, Africa and parts of Asia
FOOD Tiny invertebrates, crustaceans and algae
MALES AND FEMALES Male is slightly larger than the female

Flamingos get their name from the Latin word *flamma*, meaning flame, a nod to the eye-catching hue of their plumes. Their pink colouration comes from a diet of pink crustaceans, such as shrimps, and is more vibrant at breeding time. At the start of the breeding season, the birds perform spectacular displays to one another with dancing, head-waving and honking. The ancient Egyptians were enchanted by this bird, associating it with their Sun God Ra, and they used it in hieroglyphics as a way of depicting the colour red. Some scholars believe that this colourful bird was the truth behind the myth of the phoenix or firebird. Either way, the flamingo continues to create its gentle allure to this day.

Great Crested Grebe

Podiceps cristatus

WINGSPAN 59–73cm (23–29in)
NUMBER OF EGGS 1–6 each clutch
HABITAT Freshwater lakes, gravel pits, estuaries, reservoirs, large rivers, coasts
DISTRIBUTION Europe
FOOD Aquatic insects, invertebrate larvae and small fish
MALES AND FEMALES Both sexes are similar

Poised and elegant, the great crested grebe cuts a fine figure on the water in spring and summer with its sylph-like frame and ornate head feathers. It is best-known for its breath-taking courtship dance, where both birds meet breast to breast in the water, paddling their feet and offering each other strands of waterweed in a graceful display of admiration. During the 19th century, this species was prized for its plumage, which could be found adorning ladies' hats, and its pelts were made into muffs and boas. Campaigns against this led to bird protection laws which helped the population recover, and today it is a common and popular sight.

Adélie Penguin

Pygoscelis adeliae

WINGSPAN c.50cm (20in) tall
NUMBER OF EGGS 2 each year
HABITAT Antarctic land and ocean
DISTRIBUTION Coastal Antarctica
FOOD Krill, fish, squid
MALES AND FEMALES Both sexes are similar

This characterful little bird is highly sociable and gathers in large groups, known as colonies. Adept at swimming, it can dive to depths of 180m (590ft) and can stay under water for extremely long periods. Despite consuming large amounts of food, this penguin doesn't have any teeth; instead it has a barbed tongue on the roof of its mouth: an effective tool when dealing with slippery prey. A huge colony of 18,000 Adélie penguins suffered a catastrophic breeding season in 2017 when only two chicks survived. Conservationists are calling for restrictions to fishing to allow the population to recover.

Bullfinch

Pyrrhula pyrrhula

WINGSPAN 22–29cm (9–11in) / 15cm (6in)
NUMBER OF EGGS 1–3 clutches of 4–5 eggs
HABITAT Woodland, scrub, orchards, hedgerows and gardens
DISTRIBUTION Europe and temperate Asia
FOOD Berries, seeds, soft buds and shoots, and insects
MALES AND FEMALES Males have a much pinker underside and
greyer back than the females, which are browner and duller

A sturdy and elusive bird, the bullfinch loves to nestle in
dense undergrowth. Its shy nature means it can be hard to
spot, and it has a quiet warble to match. A fan of fruit trees,
it was once considered the gardener's pest as it can consume
up to 30 buds a minute! It is thought that the bullfinch's
name comes from its large head and stocky shape, but it
could also have derived from its old name of 'bud-finch' after
its fondness for fruit-tree buds. It sometimes visits garden
bird tables, where you might be lucky enough to see one.

Toco Toucan

Ramphastos toco

WINGSPAN c.64cm (25in) long
NUMBER OF EGGS 2–4 each clutch
HABITAT Lowland rainforest and tropical forest borders
DISTRIBUTION South America, Central America and the Caribbean
FOOD Fruit, eggs, insects
MALES AND FEMALES Male is larger than the female

Best-known for its enormous and vibrant beak, which measures around one-third the length of its body, the toucan uses this impressive feature to scare other birds, for mating and to feed. Despite its size, the beak is incredibly light as it's made of keratin, the same substance in human nails and hair. A poor flier, the toucan has small wings and prefers to hop from branch to branch, using its super-sharp claws to secure a firm grip. Sacred to the Incas, this glorious bird was often used as a totem and a guide for seers and mystics who wished to travel to the spirit realms.

Spectacled Eider

Somateria mollissima

WINGSPAN 80–108cm (31–42in) / 50–71cm (20–28in)
NUMBER OF EGGS 1–14 each clutch
HABITAT Coastal islands and rocks along the shoreline
DISTRIBUTION Europe, North America and Eastern Siberia
FOOD Molluscs (especially mussels), crustaceans, sea urchins and other aquatic invertebrates
MALES AND FEMALES Males are black and white with green neck patches; females are brown all over

These powerful, fast-flying sea ducks have a very distinctive head shape and colouration. Their scientific name comes from the ancient Greek *somatos*, meaning body, and *erion*, meaning wool, which is no surprise as these sturdy birds are equipped with the best insulation in the form of soft, downy feathers to keep the chill of the ocean waters at bay. Such is the warmth of this down, it was often used to stuff pillows and quilts (eiderdowns), and the birds also line their nests with it. St Cuthbert is recorded as befriending eiders during his solitude on Lindisfarne in the 7th century, giving them the name of St Cuthbert's duck.

American Goldfinch

Spinus tristis

WINGSPAN 19–22cm (7–8in) / 11–14cm (4–5in)

NUMBER OF EGGS 4–6 each clutch

HABITAT Open woodlands, gardens, fields, roadsides and in long grasses

DISTRIBUTION North America, Canada and parts of Mexico

FOOD Seeds, twig bark, maple sap and buds

MALES AND FEMALES The breeding plumage of the male is much brighter and more colourful than the female; both are browner and more similar in winter

During spring and early summer, the plumage of the male finch turns a bright sunshine yellow with an obvious black cap and black wings with white stripes, a stark contrast to its paler winter hues. Naturally gregarious, these charming little birds travel in small groups and constantly interact with each other. The acrobats of bird kingdom, they enjoy aerial displays and have a bouncy, playful style. During nesting, however, both sexes become territorial and aggressive to any birds who dare to venture too close. Native American folklore says a goldfinch flying across your path is a reminder to live life to the full.

Arctic Tern

Sterna paradisaea

WINGSPAN 75–85cm (30–33in) / 33–35cm (13–14in)
NUMBER OF EGGS 1–3 each clutch
HABITAT Islands, tundra, rocky beaches and boreal forests
DISTRIBUTION Arctic and sub-Arctic regions of Europe, Asia, and North America. Large colonies are found in Greenland and Iceland
FOOD Small fish (such as sandeels), crustaceans and sometimes insects
MALES AND FEMALES Almost identical

Also known as the 'sea swallow', this small but powerful bird puts in the air miles, travelling around 25,000 miles each year from the Artic to Antarctica and back again. Often returning to the spot where they were first born, these clever creatures nest in sand or shingle on the ground (their eggs are supremely camouflaged), with both parents taking responsibility for nurturing their young. When feeding, the tern hovers in the air before plunging deep into the ocean to catch its prey. Beware straying into Arctic tern breeding territory – they have been known to dive-bomb intruders and give them a nasty bash on the head.

Kakapo

Strigops habroptila

WINGSPAN c.60cm (24in) long
NUMBER OF EGGS 1–3 eggs every 5 years (with the ripening of the rimu fruit)
HABITAT Forests, scrublands, coastal areas
DISTRIBUTION A few forested islands of New Zealand
FOOD Leaves, stems, roots, fruit, bark and seeds
MALES AND FEMALES The female has a longer, narrower beak than the male; her head is less domed and her plumage duller

The very rare and nocturnal kakapo, or 'owl parrot' as it is often called, is the only flightless parrot in the world. Its circular-shaped facial disc gives it an owlish look. The name itself comes from the Maori *kaka* for parrot, and *po* for night. The Maori considered it to be delicacy and would eat the meat and use the skin with the feathers still attached to make cloaks and capes. Robust and heavy, the kakapo is one of the longest-living birds on the planet, with some reaching the age of 60. Unfortunately it is also one of the most critically endangered.

Blue-footed Booby

Sula nebouxii

WINGSPAN c.158cm (62in) / 81cm (32in)
NUMBER OF EGGS 1–3 each clutch
HABITAT Oceans and rocky coasts
DISTRIBUTION The Galapagos, western Mexico and northwest South America
FOOD Mainly fish (such as anchovies and sardines) and sometimes squid
MALES AND FEMALES Males are smaller than the females;
females have darker-blue feet

Named because of its distinctive blue feet, the blue-footed booby is a large seabird. The males use their colourful feet to attract a mate, and it's thought that the brighter they are, the more likely they'll catch the eye of a potential partner. Courtship is an elaborate dance, which involves the male raising each foot high in the air, and strutting his stuff – both birds then extend their necks and point their bills skywards. Once paired the blue-footed booby will often mate for life. Instead of incubating their eggs with their bodies, they use their large feet to keep their eggs warm.

Lappet-faced Vulture

Torgos tracheliotos

WINGSPAN 250–290cm (98–114in) / 95–115cm (37–45in)
NUMBER OF EGGS 1–2 each clutch
HABITAT Dry savannah, plains, deserts, mountain slopes
DISTRIBUTION Small declining population across Africa
FOOD Scavenges dead carcasses of animals and also
hunts small reptiles, fish, birds and mammals.
MALES AND FEMALES Both sexes are similar

This commanding creature gets its name from the loose folds of skin
that hang from its face. These lappets resemble ears, lending it its
other common name of African eared vulture. The largest of the
vultures, its powerful beak can rip through the toughest animal hide.
With its striking pink head and amazing wingspan, this enormous
bird stands its ground against other scavengers such as jackals, and
often hunts down living prey, like flamingos and small mammals.
Believed by some to have magical properties, this bird's body parts
are sadly sometimes sold in traditional African medicine markets.

Barn Owl

Tyto alba

WINGSPAN Up to 110cm (43in) / 32–40cm (13–16in)
NUMBER OF EGGS 4–6 each clutch
HABITAT Open plains, fields and low-lying woodland
DISTRIBUTION Europe, Africa, Asia, parts of Australia and the Americas
FOOD Small mammals (such as field voles and shrews),
rarely fish, other birds, bats and invertebrates
MALES AND FEMALES The female is slightly larger
than the male and generally has darker feathers

Easier to spot than many owls, the magical barn owl can often be seen hunting at dusk, flying low and slow over grassy areas, its pale wings giving it a ghostly appearance. It has the most sensitive hearing of any animal ever tested and can even detect prey in total darkness. Old English folklore focuses on its high-pitched screech, which can be an omen for good or evil, depending on your outlook. In India, the barn owl is the mount of the goddess Lakshmi, transporting her through the realms; because of this, it is a sacred bird and a symbol of wisdom.

Hoopoe

Upupa epops

WINGSPAN 44–48cm (17–19in) / 26–28cm (10–11in)
NUMBER OF EGGS 5–8 each clutch
HABITAT Orchards, wooded savannahs, farmlands, olive groves, vineyards
DISTRIBUTION Central and southern Europe, Africa
FOOD Spiders, large insects and their larvae and
pupae, small reptiles, frogs, seeds and berries
MALES AND FEMALES Female is slightly smaller and duller in hue than the male

In Persia, this quirky little bird with its striking crown and long tapered beak, was a symbol of virtue and considered chief among its kind. In most of Europe it was a different story; hoopoes were thought of as dirty birds and thieves. The female of the species soils her own nest with foul-smelling liquid produced by a special gland in a bid to deter predators. This is thought to have sparked the phrase 'It is an evil bird that defiles its own nest.' You may spot a hoopoe sunbathing when it spreads its wings and tail out on the ground and tilts its head back to soak up the sun.

Lapwing

Vanellus vanellus

WINGSPAN 70–85cm (28–33in) / 28–31cm (11–12in)
NUMBER OF EGGS 4 each clutch
HABITAT Farmland, open fields and meadows near water, wetlands
DISTRIBUTION Throughout Europe, reaching to the Pacific coast of Russia
FOOD Insects, earth worms, soil invertebrates
MALES AND FEMALES Males have broader and more
distinct black chest bands and longer crests than females

The Old English word used for this striking wader is
hleapewince, which means 'leap with a flicker in it'. It's
thought this is because of the distinctive flickering
appearance of a lapwing in flight. Their iridescent
wings, which in a flock all appear to flap in time, catch
the shimmering light of the sun to create an almost
optical illusion. Also known as 'peewits', for their sharp
and piercing cry, lapwings are highly gregarious and
form large social groups, especially in winter.

Spotter's Guide

This bird checklist will help you to identify the 40 birds listed in this book. If you're lucky enough to spot one, check it off to keep a record. Binoculars and/or a telescope will help you spot birds in a crowd, see their wonderful plumage and identify them more easily. Watching birds in your garden or visiting nature reserves to watch them from a bird hide is a great way to start.

☐ **Sparrowhawk**
Accipiter nisus (p8)

☐ **Emperor Penguin**
Aptenodytes forsteri (p16)

☐ **Kiwi**
Apteryx australis (p18)

☐ **Grey Heron**
Ardea cinerea (p20)

☐ **Mandarin**

Aix galericulata (p10)

☐ **Common Kingfisher**

Alcedo atthis (p12)

☐ **Honduran Emerald Hummingbird**

Amazilia luciae (p14)

☐ **Shoebill**

Balaeniceps rex (p22)

☐ **Grey Crowned Crane**

Balearica regulorum (p24)

☐ **Bohemian Waxwing**

Bombycilla garrulus (p26)

☐ **Eagle Owl**

Bubo bubo (p28)

☐ **Wilson's Bird of Paradise**

Cicinnurus respublica (p30)

☐ **Common Cuckoo**

Cuculus canorus (p32)

☐ **Atlantic Puffin**

Fratercula arctica (p40)

☐ **Jay**

Garrulus glandarius (p42)

☐ **Bald Eagle**

Haliaeetus leucocephalus (p44)

☐ **Mute Swan**

Cygnus olor (p34)

☐ **Great Spotted Woodpecker**

Dendrocopos major (p36)

☐ **Robin**

Erithacus rubecula (p38)

☐ **Swallow**

Hirundo rustica (p46)

☐ **Himalayan Black-lored Tit**

Macholophus xanthogenys (p48)

☐ **Budgerigar**

Melopsittacus undulatus (p50)

☐ **Bee-eater**

Merops apiaster (p52)

☐ **House Sparrow**

Passer domesticus (p54)

☐ **Peacock**

Pavo cristatus (p56)

☐ **Adélie Penguin**

Pygoscelis adeliae (p64)

☐ **Bullfinch**

Pyrrhula pyrrhula (p66)

☐ **Toco Toucan**

Ramphastos toco (p68)

☐ **Grey Partridge**

Perdix perdix (p58)

☐ **Greater Flamingo**

Phoenicopterus roseus (p60)

☐ **Great Crested Grebe**

Podiceps cristatus (p62)

☐ **Spectacled Eider**

Somateria mollissima (p70)

☐ **American Goldfinch**

Spinus tristis (p72)

☐ **Arctic Tern**

Sterna paradisaea (p74)

☐ **Kakapo**

Stigops habroptila (p76)

☐ **Blue-footed Booby**

Sula nebouxii (p78)

☐ **Lappet-faced Vulture**

Torgos tracheliotos (p80)

☐ **Barn Owl**

Tyto alba (p82)

☐ **Hoopoe**

Upupa epops (p84)

☐ **Lapwing**

Vanellus vanellus (p86)

TOM FROST
Print Maker

Print maker and illustrator Tom Frost graduated from
Falmouth College of Arts in 2001, returning to his home
town of Bristol to work as an illustrator for a number
of years. He now divides his time between printmaking,
restoring his crumbling Georgian house in rural Wales
and raising a young family. In recent years he has worked
with clients including the V&A, Perry's Cider, Art Angels,
Freight Household Goods, *Selvedge* magazine, Betty &
Dupree, The Archivist and Yorkshire Sculpture Park. His
work highlights a fascination for old matchboxes, stamps,
folk art, tin toys, children's books and the natural world.

PUBLISHING DIRECTOR Sarah Lavelle
EDITOR Harriet Butt
EDITORIAL ASSISTANT Harriet Webster
DESIGNER Emily Lapworth
ILLUSTRATOR Tom Frost
WORDS Alison Davies
PRODUCTION Vincent Smith,
Jessica Otway

Published in 2018 by Quadrille, an imprint
of Hardie Grant Publishing

Quadrille
52–54 Southwark Street
London SE1 1UN
quadrille.com

Reprinted in 2018, 2020
10 9 8 7 6 5 4 3

Cataloguing in Publication Data: a
catalogue record for this book is available
from the British Library.

ISBN 978 1 78713 164 4

Printed in China